Asthma

BY MICHELLE LEVINE

amicus
high interest

Amicus High Interest is an imprint of Amicus
P.O. Box 1329, Mankato, MN 56002
www.amicuspublishing.us

Library of Congress Cataloging-in-Publication Data
Levine, Michelle, author.
Asthma / by Michelle Levine.
      pages cm. — (Living with—)
 Summary: "Describes what it is like to live with asthma, what its
symptoms are, and how it is treated"— Provided by publisher.
 Audience: K to grade 3.
 Includes bibliographical references and index.
 ISBN 978-1-60753-478-5 (library binding) —
 ISBN 978-1-60753-691-8 (ebook)
1. Asthma—Juvenile literature. 2. Asthma—Treatment—Juvenile
literature. I. Title. II. Title: Asthma.
 RC591.L485 2015
 616.2'38—dc23
                                                            2013032380

Editors: Kristina Ericksen and Rebecca Glaser
Series Designer: Kathleen Petelinsek
Book Designer: Heather Dreisbach
Photo Researcher: Kurtis Kinneman

Photo Credits: Science Photo Library/SuperStock, cover; Image
Source/Alamy, 5; DAVID MACK/Science Photo Library/
Corbis, 6; Bubbles Photolibrary/Alamy, 9; Gregg Vignal/
Alamy, 10; Kali Nine LLC , 13; JOHN BAVOSI/Science Photo
Library/Corbis, 14; Tim Gainey/Alamy, 17; Alain Lauga , 19;
CAVALLINI JAMES/BSIP/SuperStock , 20; B BOISSONNET/
BSIP/SuperStock, 23; Science Photo Library/Alamy, 24; UIG
via Getty Images , 27; Tristan Ben Mahjoub/Alamy, 28

Printed in the United States of America at Corporate Graphics
in North Mankato, Minnesota.

10 9 8 7 6 5 4 3 2 1

Table of Contents

What Is Asthma?

Tag! You're it! You are playing tag outside. You chase your friends. Tag! He's it! You're running fast. Then your chest starts to tighten. You cough. Oh, no! It's hard to breathe. What's happening? You may have **asthma**.

Running is fun. But it can start an
asthma attack in some people.

This computer art shows an airway of a person with asthma.

 How many people have asthma?

Asthma is a breathing illness. It harms the **airways**. Airways are tubes. They carry air to and from our lungs. The illness narrows the airways. A person tries to breathe. But the airways are too tight. They don't let enough air in or out. The lungs do not get enough air. And that can be dangerous. We all need air.

25 million Americans have it.
At least 7 million are children.

Many people with this illness have asthma attacks. These are also called flare-ups. An attack may start with a cough. Or the chest may get tight. Soon a person may begin to **wheeze**. Breathing gets harder. The attack may last for a few minutes. Or even for a few hours. Some attacks last for days.

 What does wheezing sound like?

Asthma makes it hard to breathe sometimes.

 Wheezing is breathing that sounds like whistling.

What Causes Asthma?

Why do people get asthma? Doctors are not sure. You can't catch it like a cold. You can't get it from a friend.

People with allergies often have it. It also runs in families. Parents with asthma may have children with it, too. The illness often starts by age five.

If your mom has asthma, you might have it, too.

Doctors do know that certain things can set off asthma attacks. It is not the same for everyone. It could be something you breathe in. Sometimes it is dust, smoke, or pet fur. It could be running. It could even be some foods. These are called **triggers**. They set off asthma attacks.

Do all people with asthma get asthma attacks?

Pet fur can cause an asthma attack.

A No. Some people have a mild form of the illness. They may have trouble breathing sometimes. But they do not get asthma attacks.

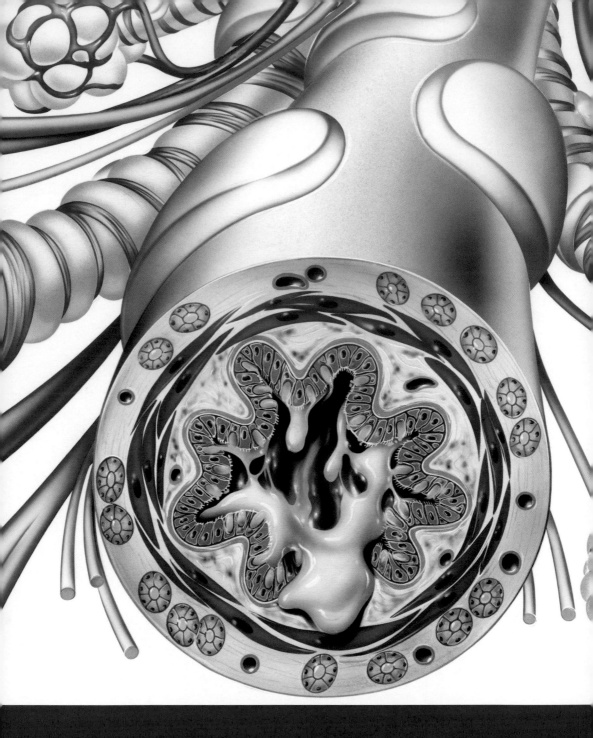

Mucus can fill an airway when someone has asthma. There is not much room for air.

14

Asthma attacks can happen at any time. An attack starts with the muscles around the airways. The muscles tighten. They squeeze airways. Inside, airways swell up. They may fill with a thick and sticky **mucus**, too. This makes the airways very narrow. It becomes hard to breathe. And the lungs cannot get enough air.

Types of Asthma

There are other kinds of asthma, too. A common kind is allergic asthma. The lungs become sensitive to **allergens**. These can be dust or **pollen**. They can be pets or food. Allergens cause some people to have an asthma attack. But not all people with allergies have asthma.

Pollen floats in the wind. It comes from trees, plants, and grass.

Some people have other types of asthma. One kind is nighttime asthma. It makes it harder to breathe at night. It can keep you up, too. There is also exercise-induced asthma. This kind makes it hard to catch your breath while running. Some people must be careful when playing sports.

 Is exercise bad for people with asthma?

People with asthma can still run and play sports.

 No! It is good for them. It makes their lungs stronger. They just need to keep their medicine with them.

A chest x-ray shows the lungs and ribs.

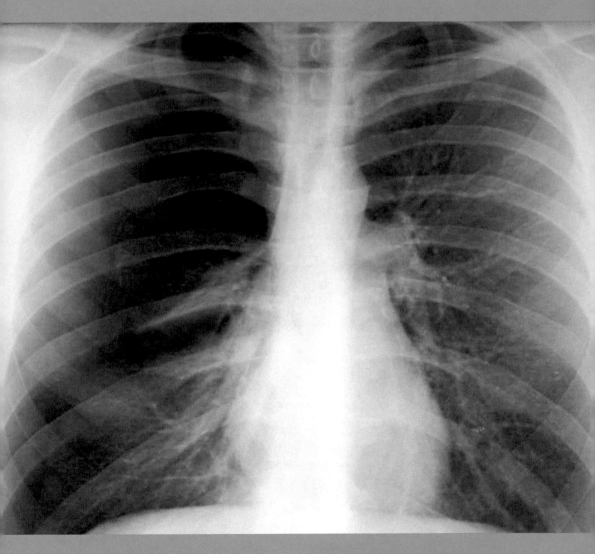

 **Q** Is breathing trouble always a sign of asthma?

Treating Asthma

There is no cure for asthma. But medicines can help. First, you go to a doctor. The doctor may test for allergies. You might get a chest x-ray. Your airways are tested, too. The doctor measures how hard you can blow air out. This shows how well you breathe. The tests show if you have the illness.

 No. Colds and other illnesses can also cause this. A doctor can help tell the difference.

There are two types of asthma medicine. One type keeps attacks from starting. It is usually taken every day. The other type is for emergencies. It helps end an attack.

Both medicines use an **inhaler**. The medicine is breathed in and quickly opens the airways.

 Do all people with asthma use an inhaler?

An inhaler lets a person breathe medicine into his lungs.

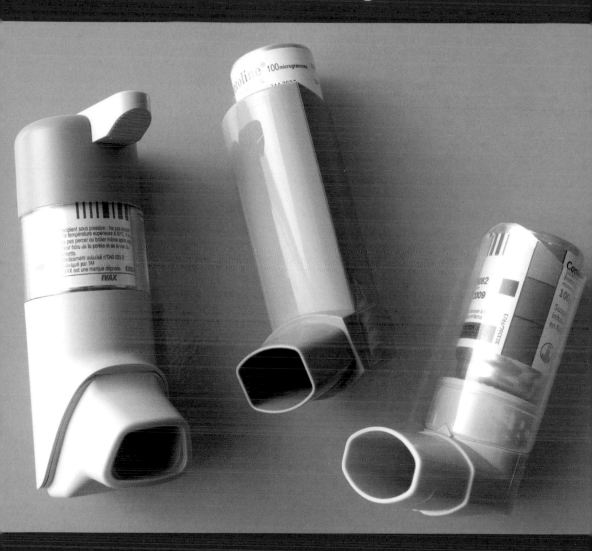

A No. Some medicine also comes in pills. But many people use an inhaler.

This girl is using a peak flow meter. She checks her breathing.

Living with Asthma

Checkups are important for people with asthma. The doctor tests your breathing. He makes sure it is okay.

People also check their own breathing. They use a **peak flow meter**. It is a small tool. They breathe into it. It shows how well the airways work. It warns them if they need medicine.

People with asthma learn their triggers. They stay away from them. And they keep their medicine close. Then they are ready if they get a flare-up.

Many people write an **action plan**. It tells them what to do during an attack. Friends and family can read it, too. Then they know how to help.

Do you have asthma? Your friends can help you!

Do you have friends with asthma? Help them stay away from their triggers. If they have trouble breathing, find a grown-up. Stay calm. Help them stay calm, too. Their medicine will make them better.

Asthma doesn't stop them from having fun. They just have to be prepared.

Kids with asthma can still have fun.

Glossary

action plan A written plan for how to handle an asthma attack and prevent asthma symptoms.

airways Tubes that carry air to and from the lungs.

allergens Something that makes a person with an allergy sick. Dust, bee stings, and certain foods are common allergens.

asthma A breathing illness of the airways.

inhaler A tool that lets a person breathe in asthma medicine.

mucus A thick, sticky liquid the body makes.

peak flow meter A tool that measures how well the airways are working.

pollen A fine, powdery dust made by flowers.

triggers Things that set off an asthma attack.

wheeze To breathe with difficulty.

Read More

Bee, Peta. *I Have Asthma.* New York: Gareth Stevens Publishing, 2011.

Parker, Vic. *I Know Someone with Asthma.* Chicago: Heinemann Library, 2011.

Robbins, Lynette. *How to Deal with Asthma.* New York: Powerkids Press, 2010.

Websites

Asthma Education for Kids and Parents on Lungtropolis
www.lungtroplis.com

Just for Kids: Allergies and Asthma Games, Puzzles, and More
www.aaaai.org/conditions-and-treatments/ just-for-kids.aspx

KidsHealth: Asthma
kidshealth.org/kid/asthma_basics/what/asthma.html

Index

About the Author

Michelle Levine has written and edited many nonfiction books for children. She loves learning about new things—like asthma—and sharing what she's learned with her readers. She lives in St. Paul, Minnesota.